I HEAR THE BLACK RAVEN

A Petite Memoir

CLAIRE ISHI AYETORO

EDITED BY AVINA PEREIRA

equalage
PUBLISHING

www.ishiayetoro.com

I Hear the Black Raven - Ebook MobiPocket

ISBN: 978-1-7373631-1-8

I Hear the Black Raven - Print Paperback
ISBN: 978-1-7373631-0-1

for all the souls

black raven
stay a while with me
teach me your song
it echoes
and leads me like bread crumbs
evolution of mind
cemented in time
gone as quickly as you appeared
your croaking lingers in my ear

PRELUDE

The black raven is symbolic for many cultures around the world. Some view it as an omen of good, others as a sign of foreboding. Some see it as a divine messenger, a communicator of cosmic secrets and deep mysteries. It is associated with the pursuit of knowledge and wisdom. It is a highly intelligent, resourceful creature with the ability to create tools to meet a need. It can represent shape-shifting, the ability to transform, and it can represent the mysteries of the void, the black hole in space that draws matter and energy to itself and releases it in different forms.

When we have an experience, we are

quick to label that experience as "good" or "bad," but every experience in life is just that: an experience. Set in motion from the inception of our world. Like a pebble thrown into a body of water, events began and their effects ripple into an indefinite future. An event can be compared to a single domino. A domino is neither good nor bad. When it falls, it is simply reacting to a stimulus. The reaction is labeled as good or bad by the person observing, and their perception of the reaction as having an effect that is beneficial or one that is undesirable.

Events are always happening. We are always experiencing life. How we deal with, process, and incorporate each experience is what gives them meaning. We cannot see the future and determine immediately how an experience will ultimately fit in our personal narrative, but we can take each moment we live for what it is and consider it a growth opportunity or a chance to pivot.

Claire Ishi Ayetoro

There is a black raven constantly appearing in each of our lives, making its utterance. It could be near now. Can you hear it? What is it revealing to you? Do you hear a pleasant sound? Does it disturb you? The black raven utters, but we decide how we hear it. We choose how we view and react to our experiences in the same way.

Listen to the raven.

Behind the Curtain

The Cast Assembles

I look for my reflection
at the mirror, I stand
I don't see woman
I don't see man
I see spirit
wild and free
not tame
a beast abides in me

INTRODUCTION

Virgin Frontier

At the writing of this memoir, I am 31 years of age. Not quite young, not quite old, but at somewhat of a checkpoint. I've learned enough to set me on a good path in life, but I still have a lifetime of learning to go. Despite what I lack in age, I have come to believe that I, and others, can become a bridge, linking a person from one phase of life to the next, at any point, through our ability to be mentors. By sharing our stories and wisdom, we can inspire those after us, and even those before us, helping them get to their next level or stage of development. Many times, we don't know exactly what we need until we stumble upon it. And that "aha" moment means everything.

I want to take a risk and share my life with you. I gain from other's willingness to share on a daily basis. Now, it is time for me to pay it forward. I hope that you will be uplifted and understand that no matter what life throws your way, you can overcome it. Know that it is "okay" to feel your feelings; if you feel good about an experience, that is fantastic, but if you feel "not so good," know that things will get better. Let life be what it is, and let time do its work; everything does not have to be solved at once.

The path of my life has taken me on many adventures. The roles I have found myself in have not garnered me any fame, but they have so enriched my life. I have broken personal barriers and pushed past perceived limits. I have evaded the crushing grip of death. I have survived insanity. I have grappled with demons and been carried by angels.

We rely on the artistry of actors and actresses to cultivate experiences that move us, but the reality is, we are all starring in our own personal drama, sci-fi thriller, or comedy; our own feature film.

I hope you will learn from and gain from the scenes of my life that follow, but first let me introduce you to the cast.

The Child

I was a happy child, and although my childhood was not perfect, it was filled with the love of family and friends. In my small community of Soso, Mississippi, family surrounded me on every side. Between my sister and cousins, I was hardly ever without a playmate.

We climbed trees, rode bikes, rolled down hills, played hide-and-go-seek, and tussled with one another. We enjoyed video games, cartoons, and reruns of our favorite movies. We took turns spending the night at each other's homes.

I was a bit of a tomboy. Up until middle school, I could be found in the boys' section of the clothing store when selecting my attire. I spent much of my time outdoors. Soso is a very rural place, with lots of open land, wooded areas, and hills. The city has no traffic lights, and with only one gas station and a Dollar General convenience store, there is little in the way of entertainment. I can recall flying kites on windy days, picking out abstract shapes as I watched clouds pass, and gazing in wonder at the stars in the night sky.

I had a fascination with bugs, particularly crickets, grasshoppers, and fireflies. Nature became my sanctuary, and I escaped to it often.

My childhood was also spent in travel. Trips to north Mississippi to visit Grandma Emma were always a treat. She lived in the city of Charleston on a steep hill and had a horse in her backyard. I enjoyed the crisp country air, the home cooked food, and epic stories Grandma Emma told.

The one stain on my childhood memory is being the victim of repeated inappropriate sexual behavior. It happens all too often and does not discriminate. We will return to this later.

The Student

High school Salutatorian. Voted "Most Likely to Succeed." A member of the Homecoming Court. My senior year of high school was one of my best, but before then, there were challenging times.

In my younger years, I was very shy and a victim of bullying. I was small, wore glasses, had braces, and didn't fit in with the more popular students. Eventually, the bullying subsided, but I remained reserved.

In first grade, there was some concern that I was slow of mind and needed to be put in remedial classes. This was likely due to my reservation and silence. I was primarily an observer, and this was seen as a deficiency. I underwent a series of tests in order to determine the direction of my education. Instead of condemning me to a life of remediation, they determined that I was actually quite gifted. I was placed in a program called "Star Reach" for gifted students. This enabled me to attend a special center once a week for my entire elementary education where I was able to explore advanced topics and activities.

At regular school, I often finished my work early and took naps for which I was scolded, but Star Reach kept my full attention and allowed me to blossom.

I earned high marks in most every

subject from elementary through university, but from preschool through elementary, I struggled with language, reading, and comprehension.

"Hooked-on-Phonics" was a program prescribed by my mother to drive home language concepts, and it was the bane of my early life. As I was forced to learn and understand these strange symbols and concepts, I experienced much anguish and cried miserably, but it turned out to be in my best interest.

After high school, I attended Jones County Junior College and was inducted into the Hall of Fame for my achievements. I was an inaugural member of the Charles Pickering Honors Institute under the direction of Dr. Mark Taylor and a newly formed group of college representatives called the Jones Ambassadors. The honors institute enabled me to take my first trip out of the country to Spain and Morocco, and allowed me the honor of attending President Barack Obama's Inauguration.

I began attending Mississippi State University in 2009. There I endured the rigors of earning an engineering degree. I started out in the electrical engineering major, but later switched to mechanical. I graduated with my Bachelor's degree in Mechanical Engineering December of 2013.

The Engineer

While at Mississippi State, I landed an opportunity to co-op with a Fortune 500 oil and gas company.

As co-ops are generally set up, I worked a semester at an oil and gas refinery and then attended classes for a semester at the university. This rotation continued from approximately 2011 to 2013. As a co-op, there was no guarantee that the company I worked for would hire me, but I was very fortunate to be offered a position, and I accepted. I was offered a salary of nearly six figures and began work full-time at the refinery February of 2014.

I chose to go into the field of engineering in high school. I was under the impression that this would be a great career for an introvert, but that was far from the truth. In my experience, being an engineer is akin to being a project manager in that there is a lot of interfacing involved - with customers and clients while conducting and attending meetings. Most of my office time was spent on the phone convincing stakeholders why they should approve my budget requests instead of using Visio to design piping systems for my work orders (which I loved) or responding to emails (which I preferred better than phone conversations). I was encouraged to "get facetime" with important managers so that I would stand out from my other talented coworkers and be considered for new positions and promotions. The environment was full of competition and was highly political, a major stressor.

I succeeded in this career for a while, but an incessant ailment eventually surfaced and severely complicated my ability to perform to my fullest capacity.

The Artist

When I was a child, my mother took up an art class at a local community college. She brought projects home to work on, and I watched her work.

My sister and I were later enrolled in a painting class in downtown Laurel, Mississippi at the local YWCO. The smell of the oil paints and thinners caused me to have headaches, so I eventually switched to drawing.

With my first drawings, I spent time reproducing animals and landscapes from drawing books, but eventually, I developed a knack for portraits. I learned how to control the pressure I exerted on my sketching pencils to produce the different grading necessary for proper shading. This made my portraits come to life.

I eventually branched off into woodworking, and my skill in drawing made it easier to transition to pyrography, or wood burning. I began using a scroll saw and router to make puzzles of creatures and maps. I worked on projects that included mechanical elements such as screws, hinges, and lazy Susans. My creations featured a three dimensional effect as I layered and affixed the wood elements on top of each other.

Some of my work placed in art contests, and some displayed at the Meridian Museum of Art. On a personal level, I am particularly proud that a piece of my artwork ended up in the hands of Emily King, a rising musical artist and performer.

Claire Ishi Ayetoro

The Musician

Music is in my blood. My training began in the womb. My grandfather and father were each members of musical groups in their generation, and when I was a young child, my life began with travel to different venues across the states as they performed. The group my father and uncles formed was called "The Dewdrops," a gospel band made up of all brothers that performed with music and acapella.

My grandfather, "Papa Ray," taught me how to whistle. It seemed as though he learned to whistle straight from the birds. My grandmother, Louellen, had a pure, keen soprano voice that could stir the soul. My father, Ronald, has rockin' bass vocals and could pick up any tune on the piano. My mother, Sondra, had forays in singing, playing the clarinet, and playing the saxophone. My sister, Ashley, studied voice and opera, and commands a standing ovation with each performance, even to this day.

I started out in a small singing group called "The Little Lambs" with my sister and cousins Andrae and Kendrick. None of us were over the age of nine. My mother was our teacher.

As I grew older, I spent more time in practice observing "The Dewdrops." When my time with "The Little Lambs" was over, I became interested in playing the drums for The Dewdrops. My uncles convened, and agreed to give me a chance to be an official member of the group. I became one of the drummers, and in the fifth grade, I had the honor and opportunity to play at the inauguration of Mississippi Governor Ronnie Musgrove.

Throughout my elementary, high school, and college years, I was part of the school chorus. My experiences in learning and performing choir music were some of my most spiritual and really solidified my love of music.

In my college years, I found my way into music production and songwriting. My first body of work was self-titled "Slim" and was a collection of songs from different genres, all centering around Christian themes, and inspired by artists such as Helen Folasade Adu.

Later, I produced under the artist name "Slim the Phoenix." The genre I selected for myself during this phase was a mixture of spoken word and rap elements mingled with singing. I released titles including "Galactic Love," "Black King," and "Inquisitive Proposal." I was also able to have a song written for me by Davion Farris, brother of musical artist D Smoke. The hallmark of my stint as "Slim the Phoenix" was a music video I performed in for "Inquisitive Proposal" developed by ECG Productions in Atlanta, GA under Jason Sirotin. It was titled "One Destiny."

The Actor

My stint in acting, more specifically background acting, was short lived, but I did not walk away from it without having been satisfied by it.

Opportunities to pursue this craft presented themselves in Louisiana and Georgia.

I had the honor of serving as stand-in for a day on the set of *Five Feet Apart* for Kimberly Hebert Gregory.

I participated in the film *Through Her Eyes* directed by Trent Lumpkin.

Most notably, I spent time on the set of *Troop Zero* directed by the duo Bert and Bertie, featuring actors Mike Epps, Jim Gaffigan, Allison Janney, and the legendary Viola Davis.

Claire Ishi Ayetoro

The Infirmed

Dealing with mental illness is no joke, but through my personal experience, I have tried to find the positive in it. I've noticed that there are at least two perks to having a mental illness:

I get to use mind-altering drugs legally, and I get to take frequent breaks from reality.

I was diagnosed with bipolar I disorder in 2014 at the age of 25. I suspected this for years prior to my diagnosis as I see-sawed: starting level at birth, as I grew, depression and mania took their positions at each end of the plank and began the slow and steady work of unbalancing me.

In my formative years, from elementary through high school, I experienced slight variation in mood. While I swung from high energy to low energy, recovery to a level state was more easily attained.

In my young adult years, there was a

marked shift in my mood variation. The intensity and duration of each state increased and began to make life more of a struggle.

I experienced my first full blown manic episode shortly after my graduation from university in December of 2013 through January of 2014. I would experience major depressive episodes and manic episodes with psychotic features nearly every year after.

The Zealot

I was born into Christianity. Baptized at the age of six. I was a good girl on the outside, but I had my share of secrets.

I was sneaky. I lied. I stole. I kissed the boys. It wasn't until my senior year of high school that a deeper spiritual transformation began to take place, and I sought to be perfect, as Jesus was perfect. But in a way, my focus on Jesus and his perfection became an obsession.

In my upbringing, strong belief and strong faith are highly admired and greatly desired, but I have reason to believe that I had taken it too far.

The Lover

My love life has largely been one of repression, confusion, and slamming doors.

I was determined to be married before age 25. In the south, it is common for people to marry young, and this seemed like a good goal to reach to get my adult life started on the right track. I almost accomplished this goal in my first adult relationship with a young man. But after ten months of dating, I had the mysterious inclination to end it. He had been the love of my life up to that point, and it didn't make sense where this feeling came from, but it took hold, and we ended. Luckily though, we became good friends in the years following and remain friends to this day.

Later, I would fall in love twice more. Once with a young man, and once with a young woman. Look for more when the curtain opens.

The Founder

In the year 2020, I became a business owner. This undertaking is my latest project to date. My company, Equal Age, is a media/merchandise company with the goals of raising awareness about human equality in all its forms and building community among Creatives and Leaders for social change.

Part of this endeavor is an interview series I host called "The Real Exchange" where I talk with individuals and discuss their lives, projects, and opinions on social topics.

I have had a guest appearance from Wyatt Moulds, a history professor from Mississippi. He served as a consultant on the film *Free State of Jones* (featuring actors

Matthew McConaughey, Gugu Mbatha-Raw, and Mahershala Ali). I was also honored with an appearance from Sebastian Jones, President of Stranger Comics. Sebastian Jones has worked alongside Amandla Stenberg and Viola Davis to develop and market the history-making comic book and character Niobe.

The Author

I have written essays, lyrics to music, poetry for spoken word, and now a personal memoir. The value of reflection the writing process has provided has served me well in my quest for understanding, and that takeaway makes it a worthwhile accomplishment.

I now pass this work to you for your consideration.

This cast sums up the roles I have played in the story of my life. Each character, whether directly or indirectly, has influence in the tales that follow.

The Curtain Opens

she would live through all extremes
the good the bad and in between
in what seemed like a dreadful dream
as she rode the spirit beast
bucking wild into the day
she would hold on all the way
for where the beast was she would stay
tethered by an ankle chain

ONE

Unleashed

Manic-depression.

This hyphenation serves as a summary for the lived experience of someone with bipolar disorder. It describes the two poles, the two ends of the see-saw, the entire spectrum of the mental illness. Within and between these two poles are myriad other feelings, emotions, and behaviors that can manifest.

I was diagnosed with Bipolar I disorder. The main distinction between a Bipolar I and Bipolar II diagnosis is the experience of mania with psychotic features in Bipolar I. I underwent two manic episodes before finally receiving this diagnosis, and it took a while for me to come to accept it as truth.

My family and friends' initial reaction was disbelief. It was thought of as something that could be prayed away, but this was not the case.

Hypomania

Hypomania can serve as a precursor to mania. Hypomania is the sweet-spot. In this phase, one can experience all the energy needed to complete whatever task the mind sets itself on. Goals are set, projects are started, focus is intense and unshakable.

I can recall writing my first pieces of music during a hypomanic phase. At the fresh age of 22, I set up my production equipment in the closet of my room. I pulled out my studio microphone, midi keyboard, and electric guitar, plugged them into my mixer, connected my mixer to the computer, and created endlessly.

During times of hypomania, I feel stroke after stroke of genius; the world just seems to work in my favor.

Being hypomanic on the job, I reached a state of flow. When I experienced hypomania at work, I was unstoppable, meeting with vendors and colleagues, cranking out work orders, and marking off all the items on my to-do-list. I did all this while working off little sleep from night to night. In a hypomanic phase, the desire to eat tends to fade, along with the desire to sleep, and mine did as I became occupied with completing task after task.

I took up motorcycling during one of my hypomanic phases. It was entirely thrilling for a few months. Impulsive behavior such as buying and spending without limit is also a characteristic of hypomania. I purchased a used red Honda

CBR 250 to scratch the riding itch, but when the phase wore off, I regretted getting the bike and was impressed with the danger I could have put myself in.

When the streak wears off, the energy dies down, and the motivation subsides. The projects I was so invested in initially move from an "active" status to "paused" indefinitely. I felt that starting and stopping projects so frequently put my credibility in jeopardy. I had the sense that I was seen as unreliable and that people began to take me less seriously. Long-term success with any endeavor seemed an impossibility.

Although I'd like to stay in a hypomanic state forever, I have come to accept that I don't have the control over myself that I believe I do. At any moment, I could tip over into...

Mania

There is usually a ramp up from hypomania

into mania. In mania, the brain is on fire. I can imagine if I were to see a live brain scan of myself when in a manic state, every region would be lit up, the lack of sleep and lack of food forcing the brain into a survival mode. One of the classic symptoms is rapid speech. Jumping from topic to topic as one engages in conversation with another, as though receiving a constant stream of insight and inspiration. Senses are heightened. One may experience a more pronounced ability to smell, hear, and see. But it gets worse. One can be overtaken by intense paranoia, unable to trust anyone or anything. One loses their ability to reason, think and act rationally, and begins to run on autopilot as the subconscious mind takes over. One may also experience a sense of altered time, events pausing, splitting, skipping, or fast forwarding. There can be a sense that one is interacting with the spiritual realm, or feeling able to move through time and space between dimensions.

When in this state, I pose a serious risk to myself and others.

Depression & Anxiety

Mania is the highest of highs; depression is the lowest of lows.

I have had depressive episodes lasting several months to a year, leaving me bedridden, fatigued, listless, and without sexual drive. I was overtaken by feelings of apathy and numbness. Losing all hope, I sought escape. Not through the use of illegal substances, although it is common, but I considered suicide. With no affect, I was unable to laugh at funny things or cry at sad ones. I tried to put on a happy face for those around me, to hide what was really going on inside. Relationships that once flourished became strained as I retreated from people and life in general. Depression and anxiety coexisted and had a maddening effect that filled me with unreasonable fear and unease.

Medication Side Effects

A very important step in managing bipolar disorder is finding the right combination of medications, but this process can take years, leaving one open to a variety of side effects. Side effects can include significant weight gain, poor concentration, cognitive impairment, insomnia, apathy, and suicidal ideation. The experience of side effects makes sticking with taking medication especially difficult. I found myself going off meds many times during my treatment, cognitive impairment being my primary motivation. Trying to complete job tasks with an inability to concentrate, remember, and process information quickly became a nightmare. I preferred to take my chances unmedicated with the hope that will-power could be the cure. That was a big mistake.

Bipolar disorder is a beast, and without

treatment, it can tear a life to shreds. To ignore it and refuse to seek treatment for it is highly irresponsible, and can cause someone to be a danger to themselves and others.

the dam, well built, could not withstand the
raging flood
and bursting forth released a force that flowed
unchecked

TWO

Break to Freedom

I had a car accident.

That was the story circulating about me when I returned to work. I had been absent for four months, and somehow, this excuse for my hiatus was invented. Was it the truth? Absolutely not. Was I complaining? Hell no. This invented story was a million times better than the story of what actually occurred. I accepted this as a gift, a safety net for my landing back into normal life, but it was awkward trying to explain details of a car accident that never took place. When people asked about what happened, I lied and gave scant details, and if pressed for further information, I had nothing else to provide. Some asked details about what happened to the car. Was it totaled? In what direction was the car hit? How did you feel when all of this was happening? This made keeping up the lie difficult, but I did not dare reveal the hard truth.

My supervisor sat me down and asked if I wanted coworkers to know that I needed some space as I was getting back up to speed, and I replied with a resounding, "Yes!"

Four months prior, I made headlines in the local newspapers for my uncanny behavior and a series of unfortunate events that weighed heavily on me. I had endured my second psychotic episode, and the incident was no secret around my hometown.

Looking back, I shouldn't be surprised

at what happened. The pressure on my mind and body had been building for some time. I had been suffering from severe anxiety and poor sleep. My work relationships had begun to suffer. During lunch, I resorted to taking naps on my office floor or driving to a store parking lot; I would climb into the back seat of my vehicle and hope to pass out and get rest for my mind. I had become highly avoidant, and often left work early without a valid excuse.

***

The night of November 5th 2014, my father made the two and a half hour trip from Mississippi to Alabama, where I was currently living, to retrieve me. I was 25 and losing myself. I was scared. I was in great need of rest. I had ascended into mania over the course of the day. My parents found my supervisor's information in my phone and handled the process of getting me off work to recover.

The next morning, my mother prepared for work. The original plan was for me to stay at home alone. My mother left for work, but something told her to turn around and come back to keep watch over me.

Together, we settled ourselves in the den of the house. She laid on a couch next to the recliner I sat in, and as we sat in silence, the gears of my mind began to turn. Mother was privy to this. She could sense my unease.

"Claire, get some sleep."

I felt that she was invading my privacy. Earlier that morning, she tried to get me to eat. I ate a few bites of eggs and toast, but I was not hungry. I grew suspicious of her. *Why was she trying to force feed me?*

"Claire, you are not sleeping."

"Why are you watching me?" I shot back.

I turned my head so that she could not

see my face. While lounging in the room, time seemed to stand still. I could hear the sound of the clock ticking on the wall. As the seconds sluggishly passed, I began to feel intense paranoia. I felt that my life was in danger, and that my mother was not trying to help me. Instead, I believed that she was a trickster, and that she was trying to kill me. *Maybe she would try to poison me.*

I needed to get out of the house, to get out of that space. I feared that, if I did not escape soon, either my family would kill me, or I would wind up killing myself. The wheels of my mind turned in an attempt to devise a way to escape. I told my mother I was going to another room to lie down, but that was not my real plan. I had no intention of lying down. She let me go without a fuss. I got up from the recliner, and calmly walked out of the room. I walked through the kitchen and made it to the living room, my heart racing with every step. When I made it to the living room door, I immediately opened it and bolted out of the house.

I ran off the front steps, sprinted to the road, and ran as fast as I could to freedom. I ran until I could run no more; at which point I started walking; but walking was not fast enough. Walking would get me caught. I had to get off the road and out of sight.

I left the road and walked behind a house that was nearby. Resting in the refuge of the house, I experienced some relief. I stayed there for a while, breathing in the fresh air and enjoying the warm sun. I could see the road from the back of the house, and after a while, I noticed my father drive by in his truck. He was going at a slow rate of speed. I knew he was looking for me, but he could not see me. My phone was exploding with calls and texts as my family desperately tried to connect, but I did not respond.

I decided I needed to get further away.

I did not know how long I would be safe behind the house.

I chose to enter the forest.

I walked from the back porch to the edge of the woods. *What was that?* I heard something. Something peculiar. I began to try and locate the source of the sound. My search led me deeper into the forest. I discarded my phone on the forest floor, knowing that I could potentially be tracked by GPS.

The sound appeared again. It sounded almost wiry, like some type of technology. A spaceship perhaps. *I have never seen a spaceship.* I began to really focus on the sound and use every sense I had to track it down. I thought I was on the right path to discover the source when suddenly, I heard the sound coming from an entirely different direction. I changed course, but how could I know which sound to follow? Reason began to ease back into my mind like the morning dew coming to rest on blades of grass, gradually pooling until I became fully aware of my situation.

What am I doing out here? I felt foolish, embarrassed. I began to retreat from the woods, and embark on a walk of shame back to my home. Luckily, I came across the phone I had discarded as I made my exit. *How am I going to explain myself when I get back?*

When I finally arrived home, I was greeted by my parents, pastor, and uncle who were gathered outside after their initial search for me. I joined them apologetically, and I attempted to explain myself. They listened and reassured me that everything was okay.

At some point, everyone dispersed leaving just my father and me.

I liked it better outside, so instead of going back into the house, my father sat beside me as I lay down on a bench. It was a nice spot under a tree. As I lay there, we talked intermittently about different things. My father has a gentle way about him, and his tone was calming and soothing. We talked about some things past, and some things present, and as we talked, my mind became more free, and I became more relaxed.

After a long while, we got up from the bench and walked back into the house. I laid on the couch instead of the recliner, and this time, my dad watched over me. We settled in place and began talking again; shortly after, something triggered in me. My father would later report that, when he looked at me, my pupils had dilated, and I appeared distant. The paranoia had invaded my mind once more, and I entered a state of high alert. I had to get out.

I got up, hurriedly found my way to the door, and jetted out of the house a second time. My father quickly followed in hot pursuit, but he was unable to catch up to me. I was light footed, and I had gained remarkable speed. As I ran, I proceeded to strip every piece of clothing from my black body. I wanted nothing on me, nothing holding me back. I wanted to be completely free.

I felt as though I were an escaped slave, running for my life, as I darted through the thick, dense woods. I gained several cuts and gashes on my skin, but I did not feel any pain. I lost track of conscious thought, but continued to run deeper into the woods. I do not know how long I ran, but it did not seem very long at all. In my next conscious moments, I found myself wandering around in the darkness.

I felt completely at home now. I felt safe. At the same time, I felt a strange sense that I had entered another dimension. A different space and time.

"Claire, Claire, where are you?"

I could hear my family calling for me in

a cacophony. It sounded as though they were only a few feet away, so close. But I had traveled so deep into the woods. *Why am I hearing them now?* I did not want them to find me, and when the calling ceased, I was relieved.

I continued to wander the woods. Naked, unashamed, and unafraid. In and out of conscious awareness. I was driven reflexively, my brain and body hostage to my subconscious mind.

The season was fall; it was cold, but I did not feel the cold at all. I had no clue where I was, but I did not worry.

I came upon a clear opening. I thought of how it might be hunting season. I did not want to be mistaken for a poor deer and be shot; I wandered further.

More time passed.

I grew weary of wandering. *How many hours have gone by?* I suddenly noticed a light appear. Whether it was a figment of my imagination or a physical reality, I did not fully know, but I followed that light.

It led me through a cool creek; my bare feet sloshed through the wet stream. I followed it up a slight hill and emerged from the woods: my exodus was complete.

I found myself in a stranger's backyard, but I felt as though I had reached my promised land, like I found the place I had been searching for my entire life. I was tired from the journey, so I found a spot to sit under a light post and listened to the faint sounds of crickets chirping. The wind was still, and for a few short moments, my mind found stillness as well.

A subtle curiosity eased over me. I left my area of solitude under the light post. I walked around the house and spotted a door. I sauntered toward it. I tried the doorknob. It was unlocked.

I walked in.

I found my way into a bedroom and

looked around. I studied the items laid out on a dresser and looked at myself in the mirror. My hair was disheveled, filled with dirt and twigs. Two dogs entered the room. I turned around to face them. They showed no aggression toward me, no barking or growling. Just bright eyes and wagging tails. Then, a young boy entered. He saw my naked body, and I felt ashamed.

He immediately dashed away to relay his discovery to his mother.

When she entered the room, surprisingly, she greeted me with concern instead of fear. I soon met the whole family. They were genuine, and they showed me great kindness. They clothed me and waited with me until an ambulance arrived.

I entered the ambulance and a police officer kept watch as we rode to the hospital. Upon arrival at the hospital, the first people to greet me as the doors of the ambulance opened were my parents. I did not want to see them. I was still suspicious of their intentions.

I was provided with a hospital gown and taken to a room where I waited for what seemed like an eternity.

It was at least an hour.

Finally, a doctor walked in along with my mother. I was a bit calmer now, and lucid enough that I could engage in conversation with the two of them. The conversation did not proceed well. There was discussion about my treatment options. I resisted the idea of being treated there. I felt that even with all that happened, I was not in need of what the doctor was offering. At the end of it, the doctor issued me an ultimatum that he would send me to a mental facility if I did not cooperate. *A mental facility?* This was not anything that I wanted. I decided to play it cool to buy some time. I asked if they could give me a moment alone to think about what we discussed and to decide how I wanted to proceed. I thought if I could get them to leave the room, I could find a way to exit the hospital and avoid being imprisoned in a mental institution.

My plan worked, insofar as they left the room.

This was my chance. When the timing felt right, I bolted from the bed. I had no idea where I was going as I skittered through the hospital, but I noticed the sliding door entrance to the emergency room. I saw that this might be my only opportunity to escape. I ran toward the sliding doors. Because it was not an exit, the doors only opened slightly, but this was enough for me to get through. As I exited the building, I tasted freedom once more.

Behind me, I heard my mother cry out in a blood curdling scream,

"Do not let her get out!"

It was too late. I ran. I maneuvered over a fence. I began to strip the hospital gown from my body; then, I ran free. I ran and ran. I managed to find my way to the interstate, and began to run along it. I felt as though I could run forever. As if I could beat time in a race.

Being such a late hour, the interstate was clear. I felt the wind blow on my body. Freedom felt good.

Then, I heard sirens. *Damn.* It was law enforcement. They were in pursuit. The atmosphere filled with the sight of red and blue flashing lights. They gained ground until they were almost right upon me. Someone got on the loudspeaker,

"Stop running. I repeat, you need to stop running."

I was not going to stop. I had no intention of it. No one would detain me. They continued in pursuit. Edging forward until they were at my heels - too close. *What now?* My energy was dwindling. I could not maintain my break to freedom. I saw that only one option remained: with one sharp

movement, I pulled myself up over the rail
and dove off the interstate bridge. As soon
as my body left the bridge, a strange force
filled me, and I lost consciousness.

In my next conscious moment, I was in
an ambulance, body full of pain, headed
toward Jackson, Mississippi. I blacked out
again.

I suffered a broken neck, a shoulder
injury, a traumatic brain injury, and collapsed
lungs.

As the story goes, I leapt from an
approximately 30 foot bridge and landed on
the only soft spot of ground. In the woods,
I traveled approximately 3.5 miles.

The sheriff who searched for me in the
woods found my clothing neatly folded in a
pile.

***

The black raven visited me for the first time.
I marveled at her appearance. She had an
awkwardly shaped beak with a patch of hair
on top and her shiny, black plumage

shimmered in the rays of the high sun. I was not expecting her. She slowly waddled up to me, as if not to scare me, to gain my permission to approach. I was not alarmed and really, I welcomed the company. I observed her as she observed me. I wondered what she was thinking. *What is she up to?*

She looked me squarely in the eyes. She opened her beak and began to warble a song. A song that spoke directly to my mind. This is what she sang to me,

"My dear, you are brave and courageous. You are bold and daring. Claire, times will change for you. You will experience much woe, but you must reach back on good times, and believe in who you are. Take heart, and remember."

With that, she raised her wings, and took flight.

***

we reach to hands above
the reigning gods of earth
who touch on hearts below
where their power birthed

THREE

Humans on High

If there were only a single person inhabiting the earth, what would be the meaning of fame, power, and prestige? Say they were all granted to this singular individual. What would the outcome be? The individual could walk up to a tree and proclaim their greatness. They could say the same to a rock or to the ocean. The effect would be null. Fame, power, and prestige seem to only have meaning and context within a community of individuals.

People grant people popularity. People

open themselves up to be influenced by another person. People cast their affections on and release their resources to other people. It then follows that those who gain fame, power, and prestige do not possess them inherently; they are granted to them by the will of others in a type of symbiotic exchange. They are the rewards given to those who appeal exceptionally to our hearts and intellect.

That is the power we possess.

We can grant these rewards, but we can also snatch away the delicate privilege we have granted; it is not permanent. It is transient as human affections are volatile. Therefore, those who are able to capture this privilege, manage it, and maintain it are certainly worthy of some distinction.

I consider those with such privilege to be gods of earth.

I wanted to meet these gods. I wanted to be one of the gods. To share in what, from the outside, seemed like the perfect life. But to be a god, to get to the top, there is a mountain to climb. Then, one must survive the altitude and the cold.

In light of this, I am satisfied to have shared a space with some of them and been in contact with some of the same people they have communicated with. This makes me feel connected to Greatness in some small way.

The following are two stories about my experiences in "the heavens."

Queen of Kings

There are a few people on my bucket list that I want to meet some day. At the top of that list is the soul-jazz icon Helen Folasade Adu, lead singer of the British band Sade. Another person on that list is the talented R&B and soul performer Emily King.

My first introduction to Ms. King was the album "The Switch." I was in my

Mobile, Alabama apartment bathroom of all places searching for new music to listen to. I stumbled upon her through the Amazon Music suggested titles. I gave her a listen and was hooked from the start. Her sound was unique, distinct, and had an electrifying energy.

She made it to my "Power to the Women" playlist, featuring artists and groups such as The Bird & The Bee, Esperanza Spalding, Alice Smith, Laura Mvula, Imogen Heap, Alex Isley, We Are KING, and Alina Baraz.

Emily King had earned my affection, and she rose to star status in my view.

Our first interaction, however small, occurred in 2017. I was 27, and I moved back home to Mississippi to deal with my illness. I posted some of my art to Instagram with the hashtag "#emilyking." I hoped to get her attention, as I was looking to get my art into the hands of people I admired. To my surprise, the official account "@emilykingmusic" commented on one of my pieces:

"Your work is beautiful! (star emoji, high five emoji)"

Upon reading this comment, I was flooded with joy. I felt noticed and hopeful. I immediately replied to this comment with an offer to create a piece for her, free of charge, but I never got a response back. This felt like a miss for me, and I thought I would never have an opportunity to dialogue with her, or whoever was operating the account, again. But, in 2019, a new opportunity presented itself.

I was casually scrolling through my Instagram feed. As I scrolled, I saw a post detailing information about her Scenery Tour. I looked at the locations that would host her, and I saw that she would make an appearance in Nashville, Tennessee. Not only was she going to perform in Nashville, a six hour drive from my home in Mississippi, she was also hosting a "Meet & Greet Experience." I wasn't particularly happy about the long drive, but to do it for the opportunity to meet the Queen of Kings was a no-brainer. I purchased a ticket March 28, a month before the date of the performance.

It then dawned on me, this could serve as the perfect opportunity to get a piece of art in her hands. This was an impulsive thought, and I had not yet worked out all the details. I did not know if I would be allowed to bring extra items into the venue. I also did not know, if allowed to bring it in, how well it would be received. *Will she think I am a major weirdo to offer such a gift unprompted? Do I think too much of myself to believe I can pull this off?* There were many unknowns, but I was bent on attempting the task.

I put in the work over several days to complete the project, and on the day of the performance, I packed my things and began the six hour drive to Nashville. A few days before, I contacted the ticket issuer to find out if I could bring items to give to the artist. They responded that it was up to the venue to decide - I had to confirm after I entered through the doors.

In my hotel room, I spent a considerable amount of time psyching myself up for the task at hand; I would tread on the edge of anticipation until my mission was complete.

I enlisted the service of an Uber driver to find the venue since I was unfamiliar with the area. After leaving the hotel, our next stop was 3rd & Lindsley Bar & Grill. I arrived an hour or so before the doors opened, and there was already a line forming.

The doors opened, and we began to file inside. Those who paid for the meet and greet were directed to another line that started closer to the stage and snaked backward toward the lobby. I joined the new line and, as soon as I was able, I got the attention of someone in charge. I explained,

"Hey, I brought something to give to Ms. King. Is it okay if I present it to her during the meet and greet?"

I proceeded to show the man who could make the decision about my piece of art. I pulled it out of the burlap bag I had placed it in for safekeeping and presented it to him. It was an eight by eleven inch, three dimensional, wooden work featuring a wood burned portrait of Emily King. He took a look, sized it up, and right then, he gave me a thumbs up. Phase one of the mission was successful. This was the biggest hurdle, and having cleared it, I immediately felt a little calmer. Next, the hand-off would take place.

We stood in line and waited patiently for Ms. King to make her appearance, and soon, she emerged with her entourage. Faces began to light up, and chatter could be heard among the guests. I watched as fans ahead of me greeted Ms. King. Her smile could be seen across the room. She engaged with each guest, giving them her undivided attention. She talked with them and even embraced a few with a hug.

What will I say when it is my turn? I tried to come up with an introduction for myself, and at that point, I realized the exchange might be awkward as nothing grand and impressive came to mind.

I was next in line. I stepped forward to greet Ms. King. She had the most energetic disposition. We said hello, and I pulled the piece of art out of the burlap bag once more to present it to her. She took a look and seemed genuinely surprised. She commented on the burlap bag as I admit it showed my rural roots. She mentioned that when she was younger, she tried her hand at pyrography, but after burning herself with the tool, she lost interest. I laughed. Our dialogue continued for a little while more and then I made my exit.

I did it. My great plan had been realized and was completed without flaw. It seemed all too easy, but I walked away with a sense of pride in myself for having done what seemed impossible only a month prior.

Having completed the task, I was then able to take my seat at a table and enjoy the performance. Ms. King took the stage, and she delivered. She performed with an electricity and intensity unique to her. She danced, and sang, and interacted with the audience. The energy in the room was high. I left that night, fully satisfied.

These were good times.

The next day, while visiting Instagram, I noticed that she tagged me in one of her stories with a picture of the gift I gave her. That was the cherry on top.

Star of Davis

I was 28 and took up background acting as a supplement to an acting class I enrolled in. The name of the studio where classes were held was "That's A Wrap!" located in Hattiesburg, Mississippi, a 45 minute commute from my parents' home. The studio was founded and directed by Tammy Nichols. Classes were held every Tuesday evening and covered scene study, cold reading, audition technique, and improvisation. Actor Jeff Rose offered critique and feedback of our acting over video call.

I discovered that a casting company called Central Casting was located in New Orleans, Louisiana and that this company specialized in casting background talent. I decided that joining would be a great opportunity to dip my toes into the acting pool, make some new connections, and experience something new and exciting. I proceeded to make the two hour trip to New Orleans and sign up for this new adventure.

I began receiving requests to work very shortly after signing up, and, although I was not able to commit to every job, I graciously accepted the call to work on the set of the Amazon Original movie *Troop Zero*. There, I would literally brush shoulders with the regality of Viola Davis.

Viola Davis could move a stone wall to tears with the force of her acting. In every role that I have seen her portray, she delivers with preciseness, intensity, and without fail. She knows her power, her worth, and it is written all over her features.

In the few days I was on the set of *Troop Zero*, I was in the vicinity of Mrs. Davis three times, and each time was more thrilling than the last.

I was outside one of the talent holding tents when a member of the production team announced that Mrs. Davis was about to make her way to the area. We were instructed to make room. I was lucky enough to be near the entrance of the tent already, so I was able to line up along the walkway to the tent and have a front row view. This was the first time I laid eyes on her in the flesh.

She had a confident stride. Her face was not stern or stoic, but pleasant. She looked straight ahead, without shifting eyes. She was not there to fraternize; she was there to "do the work." She was dressed in attire for the next scene and wore her hair in a glorious Afro. She disappeared into the dimly lit tent.

I had stationed myself in the tent on the opposite side but eventually grew tired of the atmosphere. It was a dark, stuffy space. I decided to sit on the outside of it in the fresh air.

Earlier, I met a young man by the name

of Sun Myko. I saw him sitting on the outside of the tent close to a monitor that displayed what was happening on set. I decided to go sit next to him, and we began to chat. At that time, I was interacting as a music artist, Slim the Phoenix. As Sun Myko was also into music, we talked about our strategies for making it big, listened to each other's musical creations, and exchanged social media handles.

As we chatted, there arose a disturbance behind us.

I turned around to see what was happening, and there were a few gentlemen pulling back the folds of the tent. As a result, our view was expanded, and we saw that a little distance behind us sat Viola Davis, talking with a colleague. Sun Myko and I were directly in front of them, in plain sight. I was taken off guard, but I kept my cool, and continued in conversation.

Being in her presence was akin to

basking in the warm sunlight. Her voice, deep and rich as velvet, radiated as its rays. Her laughter was slight and cheerful. I soaked up every bit of this moment, even though she didn't even know I existed.

When on set, we were instructed to give the main actors their privacy, and I understood this policy. Mrs. Davis may not have been offended if I attempted to greet her at that time, but I erred on the side of caution and maintained a respectful dis-tance. The last thing I wanted was to be removed from the set. In this, I did not succeed.

The last day I worked on set proved to be bittersweet. The circumstances for which I left were unfortunate, but they put me in a place to be in the midst of royalty one last time.

Lunch time had arrived, and there were many wonderful options at the buffet. I wanted to taste them all, so I scooped a little bit of everything onto my plate. I sat down to eat and enjoyed every bit. I was stuffed. When I finished eating, I made my way back to the small cafe where I was to wait for the next scene to take place.

During the days of shooting *Troop Zero*, temperatures were pretty high outdoors. This day was no different. We were called from the cafe to take our spots for the next outdoor scene. We were shuffled around, and I was placed out of view for this scene toward the back of the crowd. It was hot, miserably hot, and we waited and waited. As we waited, I grew more and more uncomfortable. My body does not do well in the heat. Being in the heat for long periods of time leads to my feeling faint, weak, and nauseated. With my food still not fully digested, nausea overtook me. Try as I did to hold back and keep myself together, I was unable to, and as I felt my stomach gurgle, I tried to get as far from the crowd as I could, in order to release its contents.

I vomited. On Mrs. Davis' set. While she was performing.

I was so embarrassed, and at the same time resigned, as there was nothing I could do to rectify the situation. Shortly after, I was approached by a member of the production team. She was very kind and made sure I was okay. She called a bus to shuttle me back to wardrobe where I could change out of costume and return home for the day. I waited in silence on the sidewalk for the bus to arrive.

I looked off a little ways as I waited on the sidewalk. I saw Viola Davis, and she headed in my direction. She was headed toward the very side walk on which I stood. She walked along the sidewalk, and her shoulder ever so slightly brushed against mine.

I did make it into the final cut of the movie. At about the thirteen minute mark, you can see my whole backside in a mint green patterned dress. No face.

***

I saw the black raven flying high in the sky. She appeared to be only a speck in the midst of the blue. She descended from the sky and landed in my vicinity. The black raven visited a second time. I wondered if she had been visiting all along, and I just had not noticed her.

I noticed her now.

She wasted no time. She opened her beak to warble a song. A song that spoke directly to my heart. She sang,

"My dear, in the case of a weary heart, do not be discouraged. You will hurt, but your heart will mend. You will love and be loved again. Ishi, there is strength in vulnerability."

When she finished, she flew away. I wondered if I would see her again.

***

I marveled at a remarkable creature
upon my approach, it startled and leaped
across a gulf
in pursuit of study, I leapt as well
and falling short, I landed on the rocky
ground between us

FOUR

A Chasm Too Wide

"I want Victor to see me naked!"

"Where is Victor?"

I couldn't keep my gown on, and didn't want to. I was 26 and found myself in a room of Singing River Hospital's psychiatric wing. I was in the room next to the front desk with the heavy door; usually these rooms are reserved for difficult patients. A little less than a year after my diagnosis, I had experienced yet another psychotic break, and the co-star of this episode was none other than Victor.

I first met Victor while I was on co-op assignment. He was a rising star who worked full-time at the refinery. At our first meeting, he was laid back, and a bit reserved. We didn't exactly hit it off, but he wasn't anything near an enemy. There was just no spark, nothing in particular that drew me to him. I didn't run into him often over the years of my co-op assignment, but I was aware of his presence.

When I started full-time at the refinery at age 24, I became more acquainted with Victor, although he proved to be an impenetrable fortress. We both ended up in leadership positions for a popular employee network. We attended work learning sessions together, and we even shared one lunch alone together.

My interest in Victor did not come immediately, but rather, as a slow build: a result of repeated encounters and growing familiarity. As I repeatedly observed him in his work environment, in downtime, and interacting with colleagues, I began to put together the bits and pieces, clues that helped form my view of him.

I noticed that I became more excited to see him whenever I passed him in the halls, sat next to him in a learning session, visited his office, or when he visited mine.

Victor was a very attractive young man. He stood at a height of about 6' 2." He was dark-skinned, with short hair. He had a booming, deep voice, along with the build and walk of an athlete. When he was around, he took up space. He was highly intelligent, dedicated to his work, and very orderly. He was a man's man, having established close and lasting relationships with his male colleagues. I also found him to have a slightly goofy side, which I believe he tried to mask for the purposes of appearing "professional." Everyone loved Victor.

On occasions he visited my office, we

often engaged in some type of philosophical discussion. For example, he played the drum set, and was an excellent player. We discussed this once. He talked about how he didn't feel as though he was very good to which I responded,

"Who defines what is good?"

We pursued this debate for a little while, my position being that we are ultimate judges of our own work. It is possible this conversation made him a little uncomfortable as he left rather abruptly, but with a smile on his face.

As we became more acquainted, he confided very small things in me, and I confided a few things in him.

I took note of a few special encounters we had.

One day, when leaving my office, he clumsily tripped over the waste basket; I chuckled at this and wondered if I made him nervous.

Another time, we met in the lunch area. I was wearing my hair in a short fro. He commented, "I love it."

I expressed my thanks for his compliment.

Once more, we met in the lunch area. We talked about some of the adventures I had with my good friend Basel who also worked there. Victor may have been under the impression that I didn't hang out with work friends very often. He may have even been a little jealous as he expressed, "What do I have to do to get you to spend time with me?" to which I replied,

"Just ask!"

And then, he sleuthfully walked away.

I think this last interaction was a turning point. I never really developed a sexual attraction to him, but he was always appearing in my dreams. In one particular dream, I sat gracefully in his lap as we embraced, and that was the sum of it. I awakened from these dreams with a feeling of serenity. I wanted to cook for him. If I was teetering before, I had now toppled into Victor Land.

Little did I know, I would soon be exiled from it.

***

In June of 2015, I drove the 30 minute commute to work, and I arrived in very high spirits. I had been on a regimen of herbal supplements to control my bipolar disorder, and I felt that the regimen was working well. I had not been experiencing any depression, but as the day drew on, I ascended into mania.

It was common for me to take walks outside around the office complex. This helped me to get in some exercise and recenter for the day's work. The second half of the day, I decided to take a walk, and strange things began to happen.

Our office complex was located some

700 feet or so away from the roadway. As I walked, it seemed as though I could hear music playing from the radio of a vehicle passing by at that distance. *Is this normal?*

After I finished my walk, I badged into the building and walked to my office. I sat down to begin my work, and soon, I began to hear strange things again. This time, I heard the sound of birds singing. It sounded as though birds were outside, on top of the building.

My office was located in the interior and there were no windows. I reasoned that since our buildings were built more like trailers, they had rather thin walls. Even though I never heard the birds before, it made sense to me why I could hear them now. I brushed it off, returning to my work activities.

Time passed and the work day finished. I still had a lot of energy and looked forward to what I could get involved in when I returned to my apartment.

I arrived at the apartment, and without changing clothes, I decided to work on one of my wooden projects. I set up a space on my back patio to do the work of staining a wooden puzzle I reproduced with a scroll saw and began to work diligently under the moonlight. After staining for a while, I remembered that I had not checked the mail. I paused my staining and walked to the mailbox in the middle of the apartment complex. As I walked, I spotted a black cat skittering along. I thought it funny to see the cat out and said out loud "Hey!" to it. The cat was immediately, visibly startled. *Was I too loud?* I wondered why the cat had reacted so, and why it was now so intently focused on me. I shrugged it off and got my mail.

The cat would frequent my doorstep in the months to follow.

I returned to my apartment, and instead of returning to staining, I decided to take a seat on the downstairs couch and see what I could find on the television. The mania began to take firmer hold.

I began to engage in a pseudo telepathic conversation with the artist formally known as Drake and my love interest Victor. It made sense because Victor was a fan of Drake. We jumped from topic to topic. It was like a private jam session among the three of us. I was privy to Drake and Victor's inner thoughts.

As I watched tv, it seemed that every station I turned to was tuned into my thoughts as well. Whatever I was thinking was reflected back to me in some form through the content of each channel. I mentioned this thievery to Drake and Victor. I felt that the television programmers were cheating, having access to my mind to deliver their content. We talked about how outrageous it was that they were preying on my mind. I would put a stop to this. I turned off the television.

I became restless, going up and down the stairs and walking through the apartment trying to decide what to do with myself and all of my boundless energy. Having this type of energy was not normal for me, but on the ascent to mania, one loses the awareness to recognize this telltale sign.

Drake had to lay down tracks, so he said his goodbyes and took his exit. Now, it was Victor and I. Instead of continuing to talk to Victor in my head, I decided I wanted to see him in person. I thought maybe I'd be able to catch him at work. It was not unreasonable; working night hours was common at the refinery. If I was able to make it there, we could have a great time shooting the breeze. It sounded exciting and worthwhile.

At 9 pm that evening, still in my work attire, I grabbed my wallet, got into my Toyota Solara and headed down the interstate toward the refinery.

I drove out of the apartment complex and took a left. I lived less than a minute from the interstate. I approached the first exit, and suddenly, I lost control of myself and the vehicle. My brain failed to connect with my limbs, and I could not understand how to drive. I could not stop, and was quickly approaching a red light.

I rolled past the light and my exit, and I lightly ran into the next car in front of me. The driver of the car in front was a Caucasian lady. Upon my running into her, she exited her vehicle and slammed the door; she was livid. She approached my door, and unleashed a stream of profanity and threats in my direction.

I was unable to fully react. I was unable to speak, as the disconnect was still occurring in my brain. I proceeded to make awkward facial and hand gestures to get her to understand my sympathy with her for what happened, but I was not effective in getting my intended message across. She stated adamantly that she would call the cops, and returned to her car.

I sat, not knowing what to do in this situation. After a few moments, I regained some control over my body. I opened the door and got out of my vehicle. I walked up to her car and did something even I did not expect: I proceeded to undo my pants, and I dropped them, standing at her window. I then shrugged my shoulders in a gesture as if to say, "Yeah, I have no clue why that just happened."

At this gesture, her attitude did a 180. She appeared stricken with shame, and possibly fear. She seemed unsure, apologized, and drove away.

With this strange maneuver, I successfully avoided the cops. I returned to my vehicle, baffled, but not deterred. I was still bent on getting to work to meet with Victor.

I regained a bit of my senses and was able to take control of the vehicle once again. I backed the car up and headed down the exit I missed earlier. To reduce the likelihood of having anymore mishaps, I set the cruise control to 65 mph and headed down the interstate to my final destination. As I drove, my excitement grew. *I will soon be united with Victor!* Or so I thought, but the harder I pushed to get to him, the greater the chasm stretched between us.

In the distance, I saw violent streaks of lightning, and I heard the deep grumble of thunder. I later learned that I was headed toward one of the worst storms of the season. My window remained rolled down from my encounter with the lady I ran into earlier. I drove on, clueless of the events that would soon take place. If I could just get to the refinery. *Why was this so hard? Why was everything working against me?* I just wanted to be with Victor.

Soon, the rain began to fall in a torrential downpour. I lost visibility, and could see nothing in front of me. Rain poured into the open window. The activity in my brain once again shut down, and I lost physical control over the car. With cruise control still set to 65 mph, the vehicle veered to the left, and collided with the interstate partition. I heard the roar of the car grinding against it. I sat, inanimate but conscious. I realized that I was not going to see Victor that night or possibly, ever again.

The vehicle then changed direction and veered to the right. I coasted to a ditch. Rain was pouring into the car and it was cold. I lost consciousness.

In my next aware moments, I was in a different vehicle. Faces and foreign languages swirled in my head. A family, most likely Hispanic, had picked me up from the side of the road and watched over me until I was delivered to emergency personnel.

This time, I voluntarily admitted myself to the psych ward.

***

When I eventually recovered and returned to work, I tried to continue where I left off with Victor.

We got re-acquainted with one another, and one day, we agreed to have lunch together at the local Moe's Southwest Grill. I drove us there in my silver Toyota Tacoma, as my Toyota Solara was totaled in the accident.

Our time there was sweet. We chatted, he offered me some of his food to taste. I witnessed a bit of his tenderness.

I could honestly see myself dating him. He reminded me strongly of how my dad and uncles might have been when they were his age. I thought he could surely fit into my family.

It came time for Victor to move into a different position. He relocated to another building on the other side of the refinery. We were no longer so close in proximity, but I believed our budding friendship could still survive.

There was a special exhibit at the Mobile Museum of Art. The idea spontaneously popped into my head to ask him to go and see it with me. I knew it was a big risk, but I wanted to spend more time with him and get to know more about his world. I mustered the courage to go to his new office and extend the invitation. I asked and he said yes, but when I texted him later to confirm, I never received a response.

What the hell did I miss? To me, all the stars were aligned. Had I somehow mistaken the signs? Did my forwardness deter him? I felt as though I was baited, caught, and thrown back into the sea. It seemed that a mutual love relationship would never come to me. Maybe he was suspicious of my numerous absences from work. Maybe he had another love interest. The possibilities were endless.

Or maybe, he was just not that into me.

the touch of cold hands turned her skin to
black rot
she stared vacant into thirsty eyes, her veil of
innocence removed
furtive words convince a fledgling mind to
keep its silence

FIVE

Forgiven, Not Forgotten

Being subjected to sexual abuse at any age, regardless of gender, is disturbing, disruptive, and potentially deadly. This monstrous act, perpetrated on a soul, can leave a body and mind scarred and broken down. Sexual abuse is a grave violation of a basic human right to control over our own bodies. In children, it interrupts the natural development of the mind and view of sex. It damages the ability for one to love and trust in the purest sense.

Freedom is undermined and one becomes a slave to the predator.

At the tender age of four, I became prey.

The location did not matter. As long as there was a place to be hidden out of view, my predator would pounce. I was lured by pseudo friendship, and with my trust earned, he could have his way. It could happen at church, in a back pew. It could happen at home.

Being so young, I was clueless, but the fondling of my private areas was never something I desired. And when it began, it felt strange and unfamiliar. I felt bare and exposed. With repetition, my feelings of being violated grew, until finally, I felt angry and betrayed. I grew to question my predator's kindness and intentions. *Why did this only happen when we were alone?*

There was a stench to his private parts. I could smell it as the odor rose up from behind me. I was age six, playing a computer game when he entered the room. By this time, I was familiar with his ways. He came up behind me, lowered my breeches, and began the selfish act. *When would this end? Would it ever end? The audacity. You would really bring this into my home?* I had grown in age and stature, and I had also grown in understanding. This act was getting old. As I played the game, my anger grew. All these years, I had been silent. I decided that day that this would never happen again. Any further attempt, and I would tell my parents.

That was the last time. It never happened again. I don't know what changed his mind, but there were no more attempts.

It took several years to process this period of my life. I felt that it was my fault, that I had brought it on myself. *Why didn't I tell anyone?* I felt that I was an accomplice to my own violation. I grew distrustful of the opposite sex, and with my own sexuality already in question, this was a further complication.

I eventually forgave my predator but not to his face. My forgiveness allowed me to heal, but the scars would still be there. I would never forget, but if allowed, time has a way of making the past more bearable.

You lit a fire of passion inside me. Then, you walked away.
Left me to engulf in flames of self destruction.
But, I rise from the ashes, like the phoenix, refined.
Your curse transformed into a blessing.

SIX

Twin Flame

Her name bears the meaning "heavenly mist." I met her under the most inconsequential of circumstances, but our cumulative experience together left an indelible impression. Even more than an impression, she was catalytic. She awakened a dormant part of me that I couldn't have known was there. And I never would have known of it, had it not been for her.

I was 27, out of work, and needed to

get away, to find answers. I had reached a point of stagnation in my treatment. I had not yet found a suitable regimen that worked for me, to bring relief from the numbness, apathy, and disembodiment that relentlessly dominated my life. I was in a depressive episode associated with my bipolar disorder, and I had been there for a long time. I stumbled upon a depression recovery program that was advertised to be complete with counseling, hydrotherapy sessions, nutritional food, and exercise, among other helpful aids. I decided to give this 25-day program a try.

I made the journey along I-59 to Wildwood, Georgia, an approximately five hour drive from my home in Mississippi. The excitement of the road-trip and anticipation of new experiences served as a slight pick-me-up and made the journey pass with some ease.

I eventually arrived at their beautifully

kept campus. The road to the main office of the program was on a hill lined with finely trimmed trees, and atop the steep hill, I came to a stop.

"Welcome to Wildwood."

I entered the main office and was greeted by very friendly and accommodating staff that registered me and got me settled into my room. The room was quite quaint. It contained two beds, two closets, a shared bathroom with a shower, and a shared sink in the bedroom space. There was a sliding door on the side wall that led to a sitting area on a patio.

I could now relax after a long drive and get acclimated to the schedule that I was presented. As I looked at the schedule, I noticed that it left little room for extended periods of downtime. Between hydrotherapy, morning exercise, one-on-one with a therapist, group counseling, and group activities, my days would be full, but I was ready for this change.

It is commonly advised to enter into a scenario with intention and expectation. To know what one is wanting to receive from the experience at the outset. In doing so, I wonder, does this actually limit what can be gained? What can be gleaned from these moments that can only be experienced once? Instead of being present in our fullest capacity, we can become so laser focused on the one thing that we believe will be critical to attaining our goal only to find that what was provided did not meet our need. What if the insight we needed was actually there, but because of our closed-mindedness, it was completely missed? Unnoticed. Un-processed. This happens when we don't allow ourselves to fully live-out the experience, with an open mind and an open heart. If only we could retain a posture of child-like permeability throughout life. How much more would we personally evolve?

I Hear the Black Raven

"Hello, my name is Kanoe. I will be your art instructor. Please introduce yourselves."

We sat on the floor of the room cross-legged in an informal circle, our focus on the instructor, Kanoe.

Her smile was pleasant. Her skin was a deep brown tan. She was a native of Palau, an island country in the western Pacific Ocean. Her hair was black and styled in a very short pixie cut. Her eyes were soft and intense. Her voice, calming, melodic, and animated. In her mid 20's, she gave off an air of quiet confidence. She stood at a height of 5' 4" with a very feminine, sculpted, athletic build. She was small, but the magnitude of her personality, character, and poise was mountainous.

The assignment that day was a painting project designed to help us with our self-expression. Many of our art activities revolved around this topic, and through our

102

projects, we got to explore ourselves.

In addition to exploring myself, I became increasingly drawn to explore her as well.

Initially, she was just another woman. She made a good impression, but I had no attachment. Then, she became a teacher. Then a friend. Then a confidant. Then an enigma.

In the beginning, our main interaction involved "talks over art-ing." We were always in small groups so we were not so far separated during the sessions. We chatted about our likes and dislikes, different approaches to life, our ambitions. We shared musical interests. There were very few topics that were off limits. We had more in common than I ever had with another person, but she was also opposite of me in several complementary ways. I was introverted, she was extroverted. She was very in touch with her feminine side, I was struggling in that department. She was outspoken and blunt, I was more quiet, reserved, and mysterious (as she commented). I found her to be very learned, open and self aware with a keen and child-like sense of curiosity. We were able to share our experiences and learn deep insights from one another. For someone so young, she had much wisdom, but she was also strong-willed, foolhardy, and stubborn. She had a unique swagger about her and a sexiness that was hard to ignore.

I recall three of the times Kanoe and I shared a space alone together. One day, I was the only one to show up for the art session. It was quiet, so we took turns sharing music on our phones, and we painted. Being alone with her, I felt such tranquility.

The time was nearing for my departure. I was taken by surprise when suddenly, she lay her head to my chest and expressed her sadness that I was leaving. I placed my hand on her head and offered words to lighten the mood so that we could continue to enjoy our time together. She began to smile and laugh. At this point, I felt that I was like a sister figure for her, and that is what I tried to maintain, but it was increasingly more difficult to see her in such a platonic way.

Another evening, she invited me to her room to discuss what I was learning from the depression recovery sessions. I sat on one of the beds, and she sat next to me. When she sat next to me, I found myself getting nervous, but it was a feeling I welcomed. I read her excerpts from the curriculum and she listened intently. Afterward, she began to introduce me to what she had been learning from the motivational speaker Tony Robbins.

On another occasion, she visited my room and showed up with a coconut. We walked out to the patio. She took the coconut in one hand and a medium sized knife in the other and proceeded to show me how to crack it open. In two or three quick strikes of the coconut, she removed the shell and we enjoyed the milk inside.

At the beginning, I was the only person in a bedroom built for two. When I was assigned a roommate, I was surprised to find my roommate was Kanoe's aunt who'd had a big part in raising her. Her aunt was terminally ill with cancer and came to the campus for what Kanoe considered a "last effort" treatment. With her aunt being a mother-figure in her life, Kanoe felt a great responsibility to take on the duty of primary caretaker for the entirety of her stay. Kanoe and I became a type of team in taking care of her aunt. I did all I could to make her aunt comfortable while I was with her. In a sense, she became my aunt too.

Before this, I only saw Kanoe once or twice a week in art class and at other random moments. When her aunt became my roommate, I began to see and interact with her several times a day. With this increased interaction, I witnessed another, deeper side of Kanoe. Her intense passion, her palpable energy, her leadership, dedication, attentiveness, bravery, sacrifice... I could go on. I became inspired and enamored by her.

Kanoe was dedicated to making her aunt's stay the best it could possibly be. Upon her aunt's arrival at the center, Kanoe had a friend shave her head to match her aunt's who lost her hair due to cancer treatments. Kanoe was often involved in a charming act of dancing or singing to lift her aunt's spirits. On several occasions, she even spent the night on the floor of our room, in case her aunt was in need. She gave her aunt motivational talks to encourage her to keep going, keep fighting. I was a witness to the rawness of the relationship they shared and to every challenge they faced while at the facility. There were many sad times. Times when Kanoe didn't know what to do or how to proceed in making decisions about her aunt's treatment, but she was persistent.

Kanoe treated me in such a way as I had never been treated, and I was able to get to know her in a way that I had never known anyone before. She treated me with such kindness and open interest, and she made me feel like I was the only one in the room. I had experienced such a rare gem; she was so perfect in her imperfection. When she was next to me, my heart raced in the midst of our tension. *What is happening to me? Why am I feeling this way?* This was something new. I had no words to describe it and I still do not to this day, but it led to a process of awakening, despair, and then pursuit.

I was awakened to my humanity. I was awakened to a new sense of what it means to have passion. I was awakened to deep desire. I was awakened to love. I can't remember a time before when I felt so alive and present. Invigoration. Elation. Raw acceptance. The power of this connection was not foreseen, and I have not felt such a connection since.

But soon, our close friendship would end.

The day came when the retreat was over, and I was to head home. I promised myself that I would not cry when we said our goodbyes, nor would I look back. And I didn't, for a while. I was determined to take all of the things I learned at the retreat and the wonderful relationships I developed and use that momentum to get my life back on track. And I did, but in my absence from Wildwood, and more specifically Kanoe, I discovered a gaping hole in my soul that went unfilled for a long time ahead.

There are people that enter our lives and then leave with little notice. There are also people who enter our lives, make an impact, and when they leave we are hurt, but we eventually recover. Then, there are people who enter our lives that affect us so profoundly, we can never return to who we were before. We are forced to grow and evolve or lose ourselves. I almost lost myself over Kanoe.

After I returned home, we stayed in touch for a while. Her aunt passed a little time after I returned, and she called to inform me. This was very upsetting for both of us, but especially for Kanoe. It was a major disruption in her world.

I had the rare chance to see her one last time while I was on a family vacation in California. She happened to be visiting her sister at the same time in an area that was close enough for me to drive to. We agreed on a meeting time and she offered to cook for me. She cooked a delicious meal of salmon, rice, and asparagus, some of my favorite foods. We talked over the meal, and I had a great time.

Then she moved back to her home country of Palau.

As she became focused on her success in building a life in her home country, our connection slowly eroded.

I struggled to cope. Some of my communication to her was friend to friend. At points, I tried to explain how I felt about her, trying to process my confusion and my desire. Sometimes she responded, but she never revealed much in her communication. She never revealed how she felt one way or the other, even after I expressed that I would be fine with whatever she said.

Instead, she became hesitant, evasive, then silent. I could not understand how things were so perfect before but now, it seemed we'd never shared those bonding moments. I craved her communication, the sense of camaraderie and, for lack of a more fitting word, oneness, that I felt with her. I had to learn the hard way that it was over.

For good. And I would have to find a way to move on.

I reached out again after a few years.

These were her last words to me...

"I know you are writing to me and holding on because I just so happened to be there when you were in the lowest point of your life. Now you are not. Move to where you are supposed to be."

These words were accepted as a pitcher of cool water given to a man whose mouth is parched after days of travel in a desert land without hydration. Even in her evasiveness and hesitance, she never offered a word of insult. Never lost her composure. Never hinted ill intentions. And even in her last words, her tone was one of sensitivity for my feelings. I would rather she had at any point showed a cruel side because that would have made it so simple to let go.

I wish I never met her. At the same time, I am forever grateful for our encounter and indebted to her for the person I have become today. I am a little stronger, more liberated, and driven to be my best self because of her. The truth is, there was more to why I was holding on and why I still, to this day, would like for her to be in my life, but I have to respect her choice to sever the connection. She has a natural right to live in peace; who am I to disrupt that peace?

I came to Wildwood looking for tools to overcome depression. What I received was an experience of joy and pain that led to transformation in mind, body, and spirit. I learned that love can take us by surprise and come from a place we may have labeled forbidden. Love, passion, and desire are tricky things. They have a life of their own, and when allowed to breathe, to take shape and develop in a natural way, they can lead to the most challenging circumstances with the potential to bring great fulfillment.

My encounter with Kanoe brought life,

death, and rebirth. I will never know if I had a similar impact on her, but I've learned that it is not important to know all the details on her side. My responsibility is to live the experience, learn from the experience, and let it be. And that is what I shall do.

***

I set out into the woods. Why? I do not know. I was searching for something. Something I thought I could find somewhere out there in the wilderness. I had no clue where I was headed or where I would end up, but I kept going, my desire to find the elusive target stronger than my desire for contentment with where I was.

I heard the black raven.

I could hear her, but I could not see her. I looked up into the trees. I looked around, to the height of the sky, and the width of the ground. No sight of her.

I was intent to listen and left off my search. I did not want to miss her message.

I heard her singing,

"My dear, dusk is approaching, and night will fall. You must continue. You must seek. You must find what you are looking for. When you find it. You will know."

Was this good news? It sounded hopeful. More hopeful than her previous messages had been.

I continued my course. I would find what was out there for me. Whatever it was.

***

they told her she was flawed
she had to fix her plight
believe the love of God
and join the holy fight
she took up the sword,
to be her weapon and her light
to rid the world of darkness
with all her might
she believed in what they said
and hoped to God that they were right

SEVEN

Quest for Holiness

ight and dark, good and evil, yin and yang, positive and negative. The concept of dualism is found in many cultures and religions. In the case of Christianity, good and evil are opposing forces that have been in a longstanding battle over control of the universe. Those inducted into this religious system are taught that there are divine figures of love and righteousness in the form of a trinity: Father, Son, and Holy Spirit. They are also taught of a figure representing all that is evil:

Satan, who was once a covering angel of God's throne. Evangelistic efforts are often held to spread the great news that:

"You are a sinner, separated from God, destined to the burning flames of Hell, but if you only believe and accept the sacrifice of Jesus on the cross, you can be saved and spend an eternity in heaven with God."

The displays of music, worship, and sermons are crafted to touch the heart and help the sinner see their need for a Savior. Afterwards, during the appeal, those who felt the "call of God" on their hearts walk the aisle up to the altar for prayer and baptism.

"Welcome to the fold."

I was inducted into this system at an early age, and I learned all that I could to "show myself approved" and help others to do the same.

At the beginning of my Christian journey, things were great. I was age six; upon baptism, I would encounter the holy presence of God and be guided by the Holy Spirit residing within my bodily temple. As I was lifted out of the baptismal pool, it felt as if I was floating on air. As I learned and grew in the faith, I understood the difference between good and evil as it is spelled out in the holy word and as it was impressed on me by the Spirit of God, my conscience. The bible admonishes Christians to go and make disciples of others in the world, teaching them to obey the ways of God and to believe in Him, and I took this seriously.

Very seriously.

In high school and college, I could often be found debating biblical topics with my friends and acquaintances in an effort to get them to understand how to be proper Christians. In seeking to be "perfect, even as God is perfect," I became somewhat of a menace, alerting those in my family to what they were doing wrong, posting scriptures on doors around the house, and spending countless hours in some type of biblical or exegetical study.

"You can't be so heavenly minded that you are no earthly good,"

They would tell me, but I wanted to be in the perfect will of God. I wouldn't watch movies and television except for religious programming because I wanted to "guard the avenues of my heart." I later toned down a bit, but I was still obsessed with having an intense connection with God through His son Jesus. I sought to have that special feeling that I associated with being close to God, and during the times I didn't feel it, I was overcome with sorrow.

I was seen as an example of what it was to be a good Christian. People told me about their issues, and I always had a "good word" to tell them and a follow-up prayer of blessing. My commentary on Sabbath School lessons and during prayer meetings raised eyebrows and stimulated debate.

Claire Ishi Ayetoro

My experience with mental illness shook my faith violently and led me to re-evaluate the life I was leading. My first manic episode occurred after I visited a religious conference with friends upon graduating from university. Many bizarre events occurred at the conference and carried over into the days following my return home. I thought I had been possessed, and surely my family did as well; the ordeal resulted in me spending time in the general hospital for several days, and when I returned home, the pastor was called to bless the house and purge any evil that may have been there. Every bipolar episode I would have had strong associations with religious themes, and I eventually wondered if religion was the trigger.

I am forever grateful for my upbringing in the Christian faith, but I have had good and bad experiences related to it. Christianity has helped to develop in me a sense of morality and a conscience able to discern what is and is not acceptable behavior. I have been able to develop a character that has made me a decent world citizen. I have high respect for my fellow humans, and have been able to help them often in times of need. Religion has given me a place to belong and has given me a healthy diversion throughout life. I have enjoyed the love and fellowship of family and friends who share in the faith.

Unfortunately, I also grew to develop feelings of shame, guilt, unworthiness, fear, and a tendency to judge others. Religion instilled in me the sense that I was flawed, and that there was something inherently wrong with me. With every sin I committed, I felt heavy guilt and further separation from the God who was my only hope of being saved from this dark world. I felt unworthy of any good thing, and if I did receive something good, it was never anything I could have earned.

Not to mention, there was the lingering fear of Hell, the ultimate punishment, hanging over my head; the greatest tool of control.

Had religion served its purpose in my life, and was it time to take a break from it, to put distance between myself and God?

A Sordid, Sour Song

The overture of my bipolar sonata had its beginning in the heart of what made me who I was: Religion. *Cue the orchestra.*

The strings began while I was in the midst of a mountain-top experience, but I suddenly tripped and tumbled down its rugged side. As I rolled into the valley, the orchestral music turned ominous, and I would find myself surrounded by ravenous wolves.

I had come to the end of my days at university. I finally graduated and earned my bachelor's degree in engineering. Such a weight had been lifted. I had already arranged my job situation, so I did not worry about being out of work for too long. I was free to just "do me" for a couple months. This was cause to rejoice and celebrate! (All I wished to do was sleep)

In the last half of my senior year, I started attending a bible study where I met new friends. A group of them planned to take a trip to Kansas City for a prayer conference, and they invited me to join them. I was initially reluctant. I was worn out from lab reports, senior projects, and final exams. I just wanted to relax. *Was that too much to ask?* I vacillated. If I stayed at home, I could catch up on the sleep I desired and consume large amounts of entertainment. If I went, it would be my first family-free road trip. I weighed my options and "counted the cost," so to speak. Within the week before the conference, I decided that I could not and should not pass up the opportunity to bond with my friends before we went our separate ways.

Without doing any research on the conference, I registered for it and hoped for the best.

We gathered together on the morning of December 27, 2013 and piled into the designated travel vehicles. Our caravan left from a Walmart parking lot in Starkville, Mississippi to embark on our road-trip to Kansas City. I was 24 and in my prime, ready to take on the world. After the conference, I wished that I could click my heels and escape the woe that trip to Kansas brought into my life.

December 28th, the conference officially began.

The complex that housed the convention was humongous. People had come from all parts of the world to attend. North America. Africa. Europe. And we were all cooped up in Kansas City, Missouri. The main building had rows and rows of seats. There were large monitors posted at regular intervals that allowed participants far from the stage to see what was going on. Areas designated as "ministry areas" for prayer and private worship were also stationed at regular intervals among the rows of seats. I felt small in the midst of the hordes of people.

The first few days of the conference, I felt like I was in paradise. A kid in a candy store. I enjoyed hearing the new teachings at seminars and the live, energetic worship. I went to the ministry area on several occasions and prayed for those who requested it. I also found a great opportunity to bond with friends over the creation of "scripture bags" which we made to carry our lunch and spark private conversations where we shared our testimonies.

On December 31st, the 3rd day of the

conference, the final day of the year, a shift occurred.

I felt a deep conviction about issues I was struggling with and wanted to put the faith of the conference prayer warriors to use. I went to the ministry area for prayer over myself.

I noticed a young African American lady in the prayer area. She seemed like a good fit for me. I approached her and told her my prayer requests. She signaled for her prayer partner to come and pray over me with her. They laid hands on me and prayed with fervor and spoke in "tongues."

After they prayed, my spirits lifted. Then, one of the ladies expressed,

"There is something about you... You and your family are of the sons of Zadok... When you get the chance, go and read Ezekiel 44."

Sons of Zadok? This was a new thing. I had never read about this in the bible. I agreed to look it up and turned to walk away. As I turned to leave, she quickly added,

"Oh yes, you are appointed to sing in the courts of God."

At this, I was struck. *What did she just say?* I felt her saying in my soul. I began to repeat,

"I am appointed to sing in the courts of God? I am appointed to sing in the courts of God…."

As I spoke, I looked at the lady in wonder, and she returned a strange glance.

I began to stagger, still repeating the same phrase. I dropped to my knees, fell over to my side, and began to cry profusely. The lady covered me in a blanket as I lay there, uncontrollable tears pouring from my eyes. My emotional act was on display for many to see.

Oddly, as this happened, I was experiencing great joy. I was extremely honored to think that God would send such a message to me. *Who am I to receive such good news?* I eventually recovered, collected myself, and returned to my seat. It was my first official prophecy, but it was not the last time it would happen that day, nor was it the last time I found myself on the floor.

Later in the service, a Caucasian man approached me.

He asked,

"Aren't you the young woman who was on the floor in the ministry area earlier?"

I chuckled and told him it was me.

"God put something on me to tell you. I don't normally do this type of thing, but I want to be obedient and do this. Do you mind if I tell it to you?"

I told him that I did not mind.

"God told me to tell you that he is well pleased with you. He said that the path is long and very, very narrow, and there is a deep hole off to each side, but if you seek him every morning, he will keep you from falling into that dark hole."

At this, I imagined a narrow pathway lit by a bright light at the end with an abyss to the right and left.

That was the second time I was prophesied over that day. This was uncommon, but I kept the messages close to heart.

My friends and I continued to enjoy the seminars that day, and finally, we came to the last service: worship. I always found these times in the conference enjoyable. The music was very moving and impressive. Tonight was special. Tonight would be a New Year's worship service, and they saved the best for last. Worship was live and the audience was visibly and audibly engaged. Colored lights and strobes enhanced the experience. That night, I was having a great time in worship, but at one point, a transition in the type and style of music occurred that made conflict rise within me.

Everyone was directed to start a chant, "We won't stop!" "We won't stop!"

The music evolved into something strange. Tribal drumming and flutes. It reminded me of music that might have been played in the time of Daniel when he and his friends were commanded to bow down to the statue Nebuchadnezzar had set up. This did not sit right with me, and I transitioned from free worship mode to rebuking mode.

I began to profess,

"We declare war on the enemy. Demons cannot stand in your name, they fear and tremble. We take back...."

As I was speaking, I was filled with an unknown force. I began to shout with as much power as my lungs could generate and as loud as my vocal folds would allow. I could hear myself, I spoke coherent language. I was aware of what was going on, but I was not in control. I was led from a standing position to begin to crawl on the ground like a lion. I was shouting as I crawled down the aisle on my hands and feet. My gait was smooth and flowing as I moved through the seats. I was taken into a vision as I strolled along. I was on the sea of glass looking at the throne of Christ. My eyes started at his feet and slowly moved up. I came to his knees, then I saw his hands on the arms of the throne. I reached his chest. *Will I see his face? What will happen when I see his face…*

"Are you okay ma'am?"

I was interrupted. A conference official noticed me, and she approached me.

"Are you okay? You are disturbing people. I'm going to need you to go and sit down in your seat okay? Can you get up?"

The force gently faded from my body, and I came to myself.

I opened my eyes to discover that I had

traveled down the long seat aisle and entered the large opening in the walkway. I got up and returned to my seat.

Wow, what just happened? I didn't quite know how to feel about it.

The next day was the first day of the new year, and we began our travel back to Mississippi. On this day, I decided to begin a fast in honor of all that I had experienced during the conference. I wanted to hold on to that experience and thought fasting would help to extend the spiritual high. I broke the fast that night.

When I finally reached home, I was still on a spiritual high, or so I thought. In the days following I continued in bible study, extracting every bit of insight possible. I slept very little, as my mind was super charged. I ate very little, as I believed I was being filled with spiritual food.

Saturday, January 4, 2014, I spiraled out of control.

That day at church, I was so filled. I lost my composure twice and displayed uncontrollable weeping. My mother and aunt had to take me to the back to help me gain control of myself.

That night, my composure broke completely.

I was listening to gospel music on the Sirius XM radio station in my living room, but my interaction with it was not normal. It seemed as though every song that came on was speaking directly to me. Addressing me. Directing me.

At first, this filled me with elation, then horror.

I got the impression that something horrible was impending. I began to take items from around the room and put them in a pile on the floor. Items I thought would give my family clues as to what horrible incident happened to me. I grabbed plants that I was growing, my laptop, and other things that seemed to have important meaning. In reality, it was all just ordinary junk. I wound up with a medium sized pile in the middle of the floor. That task was completed. *What next?*

I looked down the hallway that connected the living room to our bedrooms. My parents' room was at the very end of the hall. The hall was dark as the light was turned off. As I looked down the hallway, I was reminded of the words prophesied over me at the conference. *Was this the narrow path?* I shuddered to think that I must go down this path. I feared what could happen as I traveled down. But I was convinced that, whatever happened, God would take care of me if I kept my eyes on him.

I prepared to make my way through the darkness. The last item I picked up was a trophy with a cross fixed on top. This was a sign; it gave me a final jolt of courage and let me know that I was doing the right thing.

I ran hurriedly up the hallway, past the dark abyss on each side, and burst through the door of my parents' room. I flew through the air and landed in the bed between my parents. In my memory, they covered me with a blanket, and I felt my nostrils fill with something like a thick liquid. I felt like I was suffocating. *This is what dying must feel like.* I was content to die, believing that I had done everything that was required of me.

...I'm alive.. I'm alive? I'm not dead!

After a few moments of lying there, I realized I was still conscious. My breath was shallow, but I was still breathing. I didn't dare open my eyes, and I remained still as stone. Time seemed to be moving in fast forward and, when I did open my eyes, I saw that my mother was by my side. It was now daylight. My sister entered the room with a bowl of oatmeal. My dad had just come home from a prayer breakfast at church.

"Claire, you really need to get some rest. You have not had good rest in the past few days,"

My mother tried to help me understand.

The oatmeal my sister made was delectable, and I scarfed down as much as I could.

My mother left the room and returned with my dad, an uncle, an aunt, and the pastor. They began to pray over me.

The pastor asked me if there were any sins that I had not confessed. I began to rattle off every sin I could think of that I never told anyone. When I finished, I then began to accuse others of being guilty of different sins. This served to divert the attention off myself.

When the praying finished, they began singing; I joined in, but my voice was different. It sounded foreign, deep, and monotone.

When the singing was coming to an

end, I was overcome with terror. It was an unparalleled feeling that made my soul tremble. At least one of my souls was trembling; I felt at that time that I was inhabited by two. I shut my eyes tightly and held my body very still. I became unresponsive. My family, my aunt and mother being nurses, did everything they knew of to get me to respond, but I would not budge.

It took everyone to pick me up. I was small, but at that moment, I had an unusual weight to my body. They took me down the hallway and loaded me into the truck to take me to the hospital.

I did not open my eyes until we got there.

In my hospital room, I began to hallucinate. The pictures on the walls came alive and images projected themselves at me. They had to cover the paintings to help me get the rest I needed. That night, I entered a state of tachycardia. My mother, keeping watch over me the whole time, climbed into my bed to comfort me as my heart raced. She calmed me, and I fell asleep.

My family burned everything, every gift I brought back from that conference.

she looked downward far too long, in search of home.
and stumbling upon a leading rope, she made her descent into the deep.
traveling down, hand under hand, she came to what seemed like the end.
but with each move along the cord, more length would make the rope extend.
until she found a resting place, and began to look upward again.

EIGHT

A Foiled Fantasy

I bought the gun.

I was 29 and had reached a critical point. Years of suffering and being out of work finally pushed me to the edge. To say I was hopeless is too generous. I was effectively no longer human, as I was void of any emotion or purpose. It had taken a long time to get here. I put in what I thought was a good effort, a great try. I went to my doctor's appointments. I tried the medications. I went to therapy. I prayed, and worshiped, and agonized with God, but there was only silence. No answers, no miraculous healing, no explanation for what happened to me. I sought to do everything perfectly. My heart was in the right place. I always had the best of intentions. *Why was I made to suffer? Why was I abandoned? Why had I been made a spectacle of?* My whole life was called into question.

I wanted it to all be over. I couldn't see a future for myself without hope, without purpose. I came to relish the thought of ending it all, believing that my death would somehow bring relief.

I initially feared that ending my own life would guarantee a sentence to Hell. So, I reasoned myself out of that fear, so that there would no longer be an obstacle to finding my rest. I became comfortable with the idea of burning in Hell, as I was taught that the flames would only burn for a limited time, not forever as is taught in other denominations. I told myself that in the grand scheme of time, Hell would only be a temporary blip, and afterward, I would cease to exist and feel. I gave up the hope of heaven as it seemed too far out of reach now.

My thoughts were consumed with finding the perfect way to die. I researched different methods and ideologies around the subject. Looking for something simple, easy, and painless, I became frustrated - there was risk of pain, discomfort, and possible botching in every scenario. I was not a fan of the idea that I might end up permanently disabled, and instead of my life ending, life extending into a future where I was unable to control my fate. I believed I had to make a choice if I wanted anything to change.

The gun was unexpectedly heavy. I held it in my hands and got to know its parts. I decided I needed practice handling the weapon and discharging it before using it on myself. Of course, I did not tell my family that I purchased it, but I did tell a few friends, possibly searching for someone to call me out and cause me to confront what I was planning.

I wrote several drafts of a letter that I planned to leave behind for my family. It needed to perfectly sum up why I did what I had done and bring validation to it. I thought about how they might be affected by my transition. How they might find my lifeless body. How their quality of life might be altered. They were strong believers of faith, but the effects of a loved one dying before their time could have been tremendous. The thought of how my family could be affected was the only thing that gave me pause. I considered possibly waiting until my parents died of natural causes before ending my life. This would decrease the potential impact of my death. I wanted to be able to die in a vacuum, but I knew that would not be possible.

I stored the gun in my closet under

some old junk. I would pull it out and flirt with it at different points until I decided the time came to pull the trigger.

Time passed as the gun hid in my closet, waiting for its debut.

One day as I sat up thinking in my room, my thoughts turned toward the gun.

I no longer felt the need to touch it. Something had changed in the months that passed. My desire shifted from looking to end life to seeking to find life again. I knew I couldn't look back to what life was before. My previous self had no more meaning to me. If I were to find purpose again, I would have to rediscover myself.

This new perspective gave me what I needed to begin again.

I found that at the proverbial end of the rope, there is actually more rope. The rope really never ends.

***

I was beaten, bruised, and battered. My

mind was worn and my heart was weary. I was lost to myself when the raven appeared. I hoped she had a song for me. I was in dire need, for my heart and mind had failed me.

The black raven flapped her wings violently in a frenzy. She startled me. My attention locked on her. She knew what she was doing. She wanted my undivided attention for what came next. She settled down.

What do you have for me now black raven?

She opened her beak, and a sweet sound issued forth. More pleasant than I had ever heard her before. Her song reached the depths of my soul.

"My dear, light has come to you. The darkness has lifted. You are transformed. Ayetoro, peace is coming. When it comes, embrace it and keep it close. It is hard earned but can be lost."

***

with the flip of a coin
the drop of a hat
the skip of a stone
the strike of a match
the snap of a trap
the close of a flap
a zip then a zap
the world collapsed

NINE

Earth Chose Tails

In the equation of life, change is a constant, and to believe otherwise is a naivete. In order to keep up, to remain relevant, and to survive, we must go with the flow. We must also grow, adapt, and readjust within the stream. Through this, we must develop resilience, for in a short span of time, even the very foundation on which we stand can be swept away.

The year 2020 proved to be a time of trial. This year marked the beginning of the Covid-19 pandemic that spread across the world. Millions found themselves out of work as businesses shut down to combat the spread of the disease. Front-line health care workers were pushed to their limits. And, strangely enough, we found ourselves running short on toilet paper and hand sanitizer. We lost icons such as Kobe Bryant, Chadwick Boseman, Ruth Bader Ginsburg, Alex Trebek, John Lewis, Sean Connery, and countless others to tragedy, disease, and natural causes. The grassroots movement Black Lives Matter took center stage as more people were exposed to the horrors of police brutality. There were protests and riots. At the same time, we elected the first African American, South Asian, and female vice President of the United States of America, all in the form of Kamala Harris. All of this was in the public eye for the world to see. At the same time, each individual citizen of the world has their own private story of how this year affected them. I am no exception.

April 12, 2020 fell on Easter Sunday. In the southern tradition, this is a day for families to get together for a special church service and cookouts at the homes of family and friends. Due to Covid, many church buildings were shut down. Congregations moved to online streaming platforms to deliver worship services or opted for parking lot services, with attendees participating from their separate vehicles. All were encouraged to "mask-up" and implement "social distancing."

This Sunday started as a relaxed day for my family. No cookout for us. We ordered food from a community caterer instead. Green beans, collard greens with turkey necks, macaroni and cheese, dressing with cranberry sauce, cornbread, sweet potato pie, and pecan pie were on the menu. We could not have whipped up such a spread ourselves, and we thoroughly enjoyed the meal.

The afternoon came. With bellies full, and without much going on; we lounged in our respective rooms. The weather stations had warned of possible severe weather, so we were on alert. When bad weather threatened, our standard procedure was to camp out in the hallway between our bedrooms and descend into the basement if we felt the situation warranted it. My father was the watcher. He listened to the weather report on the television or the live-stream broadcast on his mobile phone to stay updated as to the movements of the storms. There had been little action that day. It was easy to settle into the assumption that we could relax because every time a storm came through, we heard the wind, the rain, and the thunder, but we were largely unaffected. Why would this time be any different?

Our community was no stranger to storms, and we have had our fair share. We experience thunderstorms on a regular basis, no matter the season. Thunder and lightning are a common part of the atmosphere and landscape. We even experienced hurricane Katrina in 2005. We always got lucky, avoiding severe damage and casualty, but this time, the coin landed on tails.

There came a knock at the door. It was my Uncle Kevin from across the street.

"Hey, y'all."

"They say it's supposed to get pretty bad."

He came over often during bad weather because he did not have a basement or storm shelter.

He sat down on the couch in the living room and listened to the weather reports with us. He was good at looking at the weather map and tracking where the storms were headed. His coming over was a sure sign that we needed to stay vigilant.

After Uncle Kevin arrived, some time passed before,

"All right everyone, time to go to the basement," my dad announced.

The weather report signaled that it was time. This did not reflect as much in the immediate outdoor atmosphere, but we heeded the warnings. Some of us went downstairs immediately. Some of us dragged our feet getting down the steps. All of us eventually found our way down, except for Rupert, the family cat. We called for Rupert, but there was no sign of him.

We all huddled in a corner of the basement and listened for a play by play of the weather on the broadcast streaming from my father's phone. There was a small window in one of the sidewalls that allowed us to see what was going on outside. The atmosphere began to change.

"Do you guys see that? It looks so yellow outside." I remarked as I peered out of the window from a distance. This seemed like a sign something more was coming.

"If you are in the Soso area, take cover now. There is a tornado on the ground."

Looking out of the window, I could see that the yellow had turned to black. The wind began to pick up speed. I heard roaring. My ears began to pop as the pressure in the atmosphere fluctuated. The upstairs door began to open and close rapidly. We lost power, and the lights went out.

"BANG, BANG!"

"WHOOOOOSSSHHH!"

The sounds became so loud and boisterous, wind whistling, matter cracking and crashing, trees snapping like twigs. Over the sounds, I heard my father, aloud, in a steady prayer as we huddled in the corner. Everyone else was silent.

We were in the midst of the tornado. All we could do was listen, and wait, and hope that we would survive.

I knew that there was no guarantee our

154

lives would be spared, but at the same time, I was not afraid. I found comfort in being surrounded by family, even though there was nothing any of us could do to save each other.

The tornado came and went in a matter of seconds. When it finally passed, and we found ourselves still alive, moving, and breathing, we were filled with wonder that we survived.

Opening the back door of the basement, we took in the view: the entire landscape had changed. Just seconds earlier, we could have opened the door and seen a backyard surrounded by tall trees in a dense wood. Now, it looked as though an enormous rake swept through the woods. We could see for several miles where before we could only see a few hundred feet.

We went around to the front of the house to survey the damage.

The entire porch had been ripped away

along with the roof, and the whole right side of the house was in ruin.

Our home of over 30 years, totaled.

We had been raped by an EF-4 tornado with winds over 190 miles per hour at a width of over two miles, possibly the largest tornado in Mississippi history. The storm devastated our community and several of the surrounding areas. Many homes were lost and a few lives as well. After counting our blessings, it was time to rebuild.

Thankfully, Rupert showed up alive and well the next day.

Life has no favorites.

We would build back better.

***

The black raven paid yet another visit. This time, I was expecting her. She had a gift for me. She carried with her a piece of string between her beak. *Where did she find this?* I took the string. I held it in my hand. I then tied it around my finger. I did this so that

I'd remember all that she had taught me, and to remember that she would always be my guide. She looked at me with blinking eyes, head tilted to one side. She sang a song once more, and when she finished, spread her wings and took her flight.

*

The Curtain Closes

FINALE

Burning the Fray

I emerged from my experiences with a "new normal." Just as I learned how to control the pressure exerted on my pencils to achieve proper shading in drawings, I learned to adapt the pressures placed on me by bipolar disorder to enable a colorful, fulfilling life experience.

The year 2014 marked the beginning of a quest to find the right combination of medications to restore a sense of normalcy in my life. It took nearly five years of dealing with negative side effects, psychiatric hospital visits, and extreme behavior to finally reach a state of peace; the new normal that enabled me to become stable enough to live the life I envisioned for myself. I went through the arduous process of finding the right medications. I went through years of therapy to unpack my past and learn tools to refine my future. The process was difficult, but I am now in a good place. My see-saw is once again level, and I can go about life with the confidence that I will be okay.

I have come to accept and appreciate that I have a mental illness. I once thought I was cursed and wished it would go away. I now realize that no one has a perfect life, free from pain and struggle, and no one gets to choose what struggle is bestowed upon them. I have learned to take the desirable with the undesirable.

The jump from the bridge left my body in shambles, but I was a lot better off than I could have been. I struggled with the idea that this could have happened to me, but I was more impressed by the fact that I survived the mental turmoil resulting from it, and what that meant about my character. I was resilient. This resilience would later be part of the miracle that stopped me from doing the unthinkable.

When I bought the gun, I was in a very depressed state (and in all honesty, my ability to obtain it was too easy, given my background with mental health issues). I did some research to understand what I was going through during that time and settled on the idea that I was going through what in Catholicism is called a "dark night of the soul." This is a period of life sparked by personal crises that causes one to reevaluate life and transition from one phase of life to the next. Understanding this life stage helped me to get through my depression and know that there was an end in sight. An end that did not have to involve suicide.

During my "dark night of the soul," when I was so depressed I could no longer take care of myself, I moved back in with my family. The same family that initially thought that my illness could be prayed away. They eventually realized that the illness was here to stay and rallied to help me on my journey to find stability. They have been invaluable to me. The first to arrive at every scene, they drove through torrential rain and high winds on a summer night to get to me when I had the wreck on the interstate. There has never been an obstacle that stopped them from coming to my rescue. For my family, my support system, I am forever grateful.

***

In this memoir, I use the nom de plume Claire Ishi Ayetoro. Claire has the meaning "bright, clear." This represents my hope to maintain a bright and clear outlook on life, to always seek understanding and appropriate perspective. Ishi means "salvation." It represents my being saved from the damage I could have done to myself as a result of my internal battles. Ayetoro has the meaning "calm world, peace on earth." This embodies the hope I have to live a life of peace, free from undue stress and self-imposed threats, as well as the hope that I have for others to find peace in their own lives. I have taken on this name to represent my newness of life, my change in perspective, and my commitment to self, to always progress on my journey of having a healthy mind, body, and spirit.

The raven is a representation of the inner voice, the guidance of spirit, the conscience. It represents all that helps one to find bearing in this world and to navigate the challenges that are forever surfacing.

My hope is that we will always listen to and look for the positive voices in life, and let the negative, while it will definitely present itself, fade from our acknowledgment.

May your raven be kind, and may it be a welcome presence in your life, as my raven has been in mine.

.

ABOUT THE AUTHOR

Claire Ishi Ayetoro is a creative and a leader.

She was born and raised in Mississippi and has filled many roles.

With a heart for creativity, she has pursued artistic crafts including drawing, wood working, music, acting, poetry, and spoken word. In the field of leadership, she has served as tutor, engineer, mentor, coach, and founder.

In 2020, Claire founded the media/merch-andise company Equal Age with the goals of raising awareness about human equality in all its forms and building community among creatives and leaders for social change.

In 2021, she developed a coaching practice to help others find the freedom of mind to achieve the goals they imagine for themselves in this life.

Claire enjoys life and the process of helping others learn that they can enjoy life too. She believes that we all have a part in creating a better world through the use of our gifts, talents, and influence.

To join her, learn more about her company Equal Age or ask her about her coaching services.

If you would like to keep up with Claire and learn more about who she is, visit www.ishiayetoro.com.

Follow her on social media:

Instagram: @ishiayetoro
Twitter: @ishiayetoro
Facebook: @ishiayetoro

To find out more about what she is doing as a founder, learn more at www.equalageco.com and follow on social media:

Instagram: @equalageco
Facebook: @equalage

If you enjoyed this book, please consider leaving a review on Amazon and Goodreads. Tell a friend, and let others know about your reading experience!